Kane Meets the Doctor

Kane's Grand Adventure

BY
Ed Griffiths

2015 Paperback Edition
Copyright 2015 by Ed Griffiths
Shabbat Hollar Books and Games
All rights reserved
ISBN-13: 978-1519760128

We dedicate these stories to our family and friends;
Especially the ones who love strange adventures
and things that go bump in the night...

Forward

I started getting into stories at a young age.

This year Gayle and I are writing stories for all the grandchildren.

Many of them include a grandchild, maybe a special pet and our dogs. Some of the stories, especially for the older grandchildren, take a different tone and try to bring their interests into the stories. In all cases, our families' values are sprinkled around in the stories; after all, it is who we are.

We believe making things or writing, will give better and longer lasting memories for our grandchildren to have. And as we pass thru this world, what is more lasting here, than the memories we create for others. They will remain long after we are on the worship team in the Throne room.

In some of the stories, we like to add real world events, references, and sometimes even other characters, that will catch the attention of the reader. Using them and the grandchild will allow all of us see ourselves as others see us. It is always good to be grounded both in our faith and in our psyches. We are who we think we are, but sometimes we can learn about ourselves, as others see us, and be more of what we truly want to be.

So sit back and enjoy.

-Ed

Table of Contents

The Adventurers

The beginning work had only a small sample of the adventures that have been told over the years. Each adventure has drama, excitement, good will and love… If you look closely, you might even see the influence of God at work. Here are the characters of the adventure club who are in many of these adventures.

Our Adventurers Club:

Sir **Rupert** de Browser is a black and white corgi with a dominant personality. He is an organized creature of habits, and kind and loving friend. He likes to have adventures. He has a bit of a gruff confident bark.

He once ran for Corgi President, but lost to his old girlfriend. Their relationship did not last long after that.

Carmelita Del **Moxie** is a dark chocolate colored miniature dachshund who is sometimes much too brave for her own good. She has a sweet but determined streak, and a loud threatening bark

Good Golly Miss **Mollie** is a caramel colored miniature dachshund who is shy but can be a tiger when she is aroused. She is smart, thoughtful and has a sweet quiet whine when she is happy.

Captain **Cooper** is a black and white rescued corgi/beagle and has traits of both. He is the smart one and usually is in the lead on the adventures. He is the one who knows how to communicate the best with the humans who they live in their house. His bark is a cross between annoying and Gomer Pyle.

Miss **Monet** is a quiet but efficient member of the adventure club. She is the scout who checks for bad animals who might be nearby... She has a very determined but independent streak and communicates well.
She is an accomplished climber and her yowl can raise goosebumps.

Special Guest Adventurers

Kane is a bright inquisitive youth who likes hanging out with friends, playing the saxophone and watching space and time adventures. Little did he know he would have one as well.

Elway is his constant companion, and bodyguard, Elway is a _rescued_ miniature mixture of intimidation and bluff. His bark can make your hair stand on end, but in a lovable way.

The Doc is a creature of imagination. Is he real or does he only exists in day dreams? It may be just our human desire to see the future and understand the past. Whoever he is, there is only one who can actually do these things. Many of us do understand just Who that really is.

Introduction

This is a series of stories developed for our grandchildren over the years. Major characters in many of the adventures are our pets: Moxie and Mollie – Long Haired Miniature Dachshunds, Rupert and Cooper – Pembroke Welch Corgis and Monet the white cat, who sometimes thinks she is a dog too…
In special adventures others take starring roles.
For instance, Surly and Rosie have had adventures and even Elway has been involved. In this one, Kane and Elway take on the leading roles along with a surprise guest or two.

These adventures usually take place near a small rural cottage in the Midwest. In these adventures, animals will communicate in human language (English to be exact) which has been carefully translated from the standard universal animal language.

The Setting
The Adventurers live in a quaint little cottage in a small holler beside a narrow road on the side of a hill….. It is a quiet restful place surrounded by woods. You can reach it by going over the river and through the woods.

There are trails that wind their way through those woods.
o   One trail goes up the hill, crosses a creek and ends up on the ridge overlooking the peaceful valley where a mighty river flows.

o   The second trail is short and starts behind the barn and follows the creek bed as it goes downhill….past the kennels where the Jack Russell's live.

o   Another trail goes across the narrow road and up another ridge where flocks of turkeys and other wild animals are often seen.

In the Wood

It's a Good Day for a Walk in the Woods

It was a beautiful day in the Neighborhood. Elway was visiting Kane's grandparents and their dogs, and Kane was tagging along. The grandparents enjoyed space and time travel adventures and Kane knew they would have some new movies in store for him to see over the weekend. Any way, they hitched a ride with Kane's dad and arrived shortly after lunch time.

It was a bit nippy, but the sun was warm so it was a sweet day to spend hiking in the woods that surrounded the cottage. There was a trail that wound its way up to a ridge that overlooked the river valley far below. The creek was low, so they could investigate anything in the creek to see what they could find there.

Elway: Come on Cooper, let's get going. I want to get up the trail so I can get this dumb leash off and really enjoy the hike.

Cooper: All right, all right. Don't get your tail in a twisty.

With that, there were off. They started up the ATV trail that the boys next door had made. It made a nice walk with a few easy hills all the way up to the ridge. Cooper stopped at the wide spot in the trail where it crossed the creek. Kane took off Elway's leash and put it away in his knapsack. His grandmother had packed a lunch for Kane and some treats for the dogs. Cooper and Rupert were excited about those threats. They were made by Rupert's Facebook girlfriend Rosie's human. Daphne's Chicky Feets were some of the greatest doggie treats ever made. Rupert just indicated that readers can find the stories of their romance in a companion book "Corgis on the Loose".

The Hike through the Woods

The lower part of the woods has a lot of things to do. Elway understands that they should always stay on the trail so they don't get lost. Friendly animals live near the path and are around on most days or nights. They expect to see some on their hike.

Cooper leads the group, with Rupert following to make sure no one strays. If they do, then his herding skills kick in and he will round them up.

They hear some rustling in the bushes and a red squirrel comes into the clearing.

Rupert: Hey guys, this is Redd Squirrel. I found him gathering some acorns and berries to save for the winter.

All say howdy and welcome Redd into their group.

Redd: Say Cooper, I think I have heard stories about you. Aren't you the one who guards turtles when they need to cross the road so cars won't

hurt them and didn't you try to save a raccoon who had gotten hurt by a coyote?

Cooper: Shucks, it's not much, I mean, the turtles are so small, and go so slow. The cars could run them down and not even know it.... Aren't we supposed to love and protect each another and take care of sick and injured?

Just like we would want to be treated by others?

Suddenly, there is some more noise in the bushes. In bound two deer, with their white tails flashing in the moonlight. They look so beautiful with their tan fur coats.

The smaller one has white spots on her back which make her look really cute. They look at Rupert.

Rupert: Hey everybody this is Moma Dear and her fawn Dot, I told them to join us after they finished eating... I first met them in the spring just after Dot was born... She was so cute, all wobbly on her long legs. She has grown a lot over the summer. Isn't she sweet?

Moma Dear: Well, it's been nice meeting you all, but we have to get back to our spot in the woods, it's time for this little one to take a nap. Good bye all. And with a bound they were out of sight.

Cooper: Ok, let's go guys, follow me now... Rupert, keep them together.

Rupert: You got it, Captain Cooper!

And off they went, further up the trail; they were approaching the clearing near the creek crossing.

Suddenly they hear: Vrrrfffff, Vrrrfffff, Vrrrfffff... Time seems to stand still. They look at each other.

Elway: Rrrrrrrrr, Arf Arf!

Kane: Wow!

Rupert and Cooper: Uh Oh. It's that timey whimey whatis guy again.

A large door appears in the clearing in the midst of a bright light.

Kane: Right on!

The door begins to open; mist seems to emanate from the opening.

A figure steps out: They can't make out his features, the light from the open door is almost blinding.

Rupert: It's the Doc!

Cooper: Who?

Elway: Isn't that, whom?

Doc: What... ever... works... I'm here on a special mission for Kane.

Kane: Me, me, why me?, I mean sure... ahh... yea, right. Oh, I have to take Elway. I'm responsible for him for the weekend. Ok?

Doc: Sure, Elway could be very useful. Rupert, Cooper. You need to stay here until the shadow of the tree appears over there, (Doc points to a spot where the shadows would be in 2 hours). If I am not back by then, go back to your house; but I should be able to hit that time space.

Kane puts the leash back on Elway and turns to Rupert and Cooper: See you guys in a little while...see ya!

Kane, Elway and Doc head into the doorway. Suddenly Rupert and Cooper hear: Vrrrfffff, Vrrrfffff, Vrrrfffff... Time seems to stand still. The door is gone. Rupert and Cooper looked at each other... and smiled.

They had seen this before and knew what was in store for Kane and Elway.

It's a Good Day for a Trip in Time and Space

Kane and Elway walked through the door; And into a huge chamber. It obviously was the control room of a highly technical nerve center.

Lights, monitors, gages, communication devices abounded. It was like someone had an unlimited check book and found the nerd's technical store of dreams.

There were a few windows so they could see outside, but it was not the same place they had just come in from... no, it was totally different. It was a scene of the cosmos as if it had been taken from a far distance place. From one window they could see earth. It looked so small; and so far away.

And another view; the Milky Way was so clear and impressive...

The then out the third window, a magnificent sight; A solar burst...

So close, and so frightening.

What a trip this was. Kane was impressed. It was so much better than flying on commercial airlines to North Carolina like he had done before and he was even headed to a different time. 1939. Many years before his grand-fathers were born. What an adventure this was starting out to be.

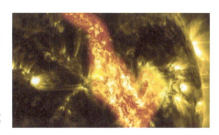

Georgetown, MD 1893

THE CAPITOL OF THE UNITED STATES

They were headed to a town called Washington or rather a smaller town just outside, in Maryland, called Georgetown. The famous Kennedy Center is also located in Georgetown, in a section called Foggy Bottom. That sounds just like our government in Washington, Eh?

Suddenly they hear: Vrrrfffff, Vrrrfffff, and Vrrrfffff… Kane and Elway look at each other. They were landing in a new place and time. What possible mission could Doc have for Kane here?

Doc: Well, here we are. I need to get a few things and then we will be on our way. Are you guys ready?

Kane slipped the leash on Elway and announced that they were ready.
Doc opened the door and they stepped out.
They were in some really dark woods, but there was a path here. It looked like the path was not very well used. Good choice! Odds were against people seeing them land in here.

Had the Doc been here before?
Doc turned and pushed a button on his cosmic flashlight.

The door vanished.

Kane: Cool. What is that neat thing you've got there?

Doc: I call it my cosmic flash light. It combines communication, laser light beams and remote control of the door and the power systems.

We need to head out, we have an appointment this afternoon in the nearby town; Georgetown, Maryland. Have you ever heard of it?

Kane: I've heard of it, but I've never been there.

They headed up the trail. Doc was in the lead They had left Elway back at the transport so he could take a nap. Soon they ended up on a small road. They headed into the town.

It was a Good for a Meeting

It was the near the capital of the country; Kane wondered what the draw was here. Why was this special mission for him? He kept rolling it around in his mind as they plodded up the main street. They went by a bank, a small coffee shop, a tailor shop, past a hotel, with the bell hop snoozing in a chair on the porch.

They were standing in front of a small funny shaped building. The sign on the outside said: Volta Laboratory and Bureau.

Kane: Hey, Doc, what is this place?.

Doc: It's the lab of Alexander Graham Bell. You may know it better as Bell Labs. You are here to find out what is happening, But don't worry he expects us. I had Herman send him a note.

Kane: Harmen who?

Doc: Harmen Hollerith, he was a photographer.

Kane: Why are we here to see a photographer?

Doc: Because this photographer invented the punch card that was used to tabulate the 1890 census. The punched cards could be read by a special machine, called a tabulator. This process allowed the census to be tabulated in only 6 years instead of the normal 8. In fact the rough count of the entire United States was done in only 6 weeks.

The population then was 62,947,714, and of that 2,192,404 lived in Indiana. And Kane, that breakthrough led to the digitizing of the entire information collection process, that has ended up as you know it as the Internet. Unfortunately most of the records of that census were lost in a fire, either burnt or damaged by smoke and water. Your grandfather knows all about that from doing genealogy. The census information is a key for finding prior generations. But, here comes Dr. Bell, have you got your questions ready for him?

Kane: ah, yeah, sure.

Doc: Hi Alex, this is my friend Kane. He is a student friend of mine and he was interested in finding out more about your work here.

Alex: Well Kane, thanks for showing interest in our work here. We are very interested in advancing technology for the benefit of all people. I'll be glad to answer any questions you have.

Kane: if you could give your philosophy in a short sentence, what would it be?

Alex: I've always believed in this: Sometimes we stare so long at a door that is closing, that we see too late, the one that is open. That's why this laboratory was established; for the pure research and potential application of science and technology. It will result in changes to man's existence that we can only guess at today. I believe that God has strewn our paths with wonders, and we certainly should not go through life with our eyes shut.

Kane: That is too cool.

Alex: Your cold here, should I turn up the heat?

Kane: No, no, sorry, that's just a term we use in our neighbor to let people know that it's a great thing. Can I ask about what new things you are working on?

Alex: sure, if you are a friend of Docs, I'd be happy tell about some of our new projects. Over here we are working on a method to transmit pictures over long distances quickly. We think if we can divide a picture into tiny squares and with numbers for each square and use other numbers to represent a shade of white and black, we could either use Sam More's invention or send sounds waves through a telephone line to send pictures across the country. Think of that. Pictures from New York could be printed in California in a day or so.

We are also doing some negotiations to lay a cable across the Atlantic Ocean so we could have telephones in America, connect to phones in Europe. That way messages, as well a voice and pictures could be sent from Europe or America. The world could communicate just like we do in our home towns. The possibilities are endless, we just have to work hard and solve the problems that come up.

Kane: That sounds like a great way to plan for the future.

Alex: I think so too, but I think I have to get that phone that's ringing in my office, I wish I had one I could just carry with me.

Kane: Thanks Sir, it's been a pleasure spending this time with you and thanks for the advice. And about that portable phone. It sounds like a great idea to me too.

So with that, Doc and Kane headed into Washington DC, it was just a short walk over the bridge to get there. The Potomac River was glistening in the noonday sun as they made their way to see the sights. Fortunately the trolley came along so they could get around and see the sights in style.

They checked out the new Washington Monument. It looked so strange

to the pictures Kane had seen in magazines and on Television.

Kane: Look at the Monument; Its two different colors and it's in water. What's up with that?

Doc: Well the story is, that they picked a cheap property to build it on and then ran out of money to finish it. That's the dark portion of the monument. Then they had a fund drive across the country using schools to collected pennies from school kids. That provided the money to finish the monument and then they fixed the flooding issue. You could climb the stairs after it's fixed, but today, I don't think it is even open. Notice how sparse everything is.

The city grows a lot, we'll be back here in 1947, but that's the next stop. We have to talk with another key figure in our internet search. They continued their sightseeing: They saw the Lincoln Memorial being built. Then there was the capital building; it looked so grand. Next Stop: 1965, in New York City: we're going to the fair. THE FAIR.

It's a Good Day for a Trip in Time and Space

Kane and Doc made it back to Elway, who was excited to see them. He barked and squiggled around until Kane brought out a hot dog that he had picked up from a vender on the Washington Mall. Elway got right to work on that delicacy. Afterwards, Kane slipped the leash on Elway and took him out for normal his after dinner constitutional.

Kane and Elway came back in and Kane said that Elway had gone and was now go to go.

Doc: Well it's time for us to head out to 1965. We have to see how scientist are projecting uses of some of what you have seen.

Vrrrfffff, Vrrrfffff, Vrrrfffff ... Time seems to stand still. The door is gone.

Kane was glued to the window; what would he see this time. now it changed and according to Doc:

it was the Carina Nebula...
or the Pillars of Creation.

Then the view changed again; The Veil Nebula. Awesome!

Believe it or not, Kane took a quick nap on this leg of the trip, he knew that there were more stops on the way and he wanted to be ready for them.

New York City 1965

A Good Day for the Fair

Somewhere in an alley between abandoned buildings in Flushing New York, a blue door appeared on the side of one of the buildings. Elway was asleep, so Doc told Kane to let him sleep, Elway would not be able to go with them this time.

They slipped out the door; Doc pushed a button on the cosmic flashlight and the door disappeared.

Kane: Hey where are we now? This is still not Indiana.

Doc: Nothing gets by you Kane. Didn't I tell you we were going to the fair? The Fair. The New York World's Fair. It's now 1965.

It is the largest fair in the world right now, and this is the second year. You are going to love it...

Doc: Well Kane, what do you think of this walk way? Check out the Unisphere at the end. That's what is "blown up" in the movie.

You've probably seen the symbol of it in the "Men in Black" movie. There was a terrific scene with it, remember?

Kane: Yea I saw that, you mean we're going there, cool.

Off they go, Doc changes some currency with his cosmic flashlight so they can get in and do all the stuff that normal fair goers do. Now we are not going to relate every moment of that day, but there were some very neat exhibits there. Many nations in the world as well as a number of states, and corporations were represented.

Doc: As we walk to the entrance, check out that ball park over there. It's the new Met's stadium, Casey Stengel; the old manager of the Yankees is their first coach. The team couldn't get any stars so they are losing a ton of games. They have a huge fan base, everybody loves an underdog.

The first thing we are going to do is to walk down the avenue of nations, it is a majestic walk with exhibits, fountains and trees all around, you'll see.

Now we're off to see a bunch of the corporate and state exhibits.

"Great moments with Mr. Lincoln", the exhibit for the state of Illinois, has a life sized robotic model of Abraham Lincoln who moves, gives the Gettysburg Address... it is very realistic.

Next we have the Pepsi's UNICEF Exhibit; it's a boat ride about
"It's a small, small world". It has portrayals of scenes from countries all over the world with dolls moving and "singing" the song in different languages. It's a good ride to take when you get tired from all the walking.

And over there is the GE *"Carousel of Progress"* pavilion. It shows the inventions progressing over the ages, from homes in colonial times to

the future times when computers help do all the work in a home. Kane, you have most of them in your home now, but they did not exist in 1965.

Disney had a deal with many of these companies to build exhibits and then move them to a town in Florida, called Bay Lake, near Kissimmee and build a new park called Disney World. If you haven't been there, you probably will, most people do seem to make it there at some time in their life.

One of the Fair's most popular exhibits was the Vatican pavilion where Michelangelo's 465-year-old masterpiece in carved Carrara marble, the Pietà was displayed. Since it was installed in Old St. Peter's

Basilica in 1499, it had never left the Vatican until this World's Fair.

Doc: I liked the recreation of the medieval Belgian Village and especially the new taste sensation in the form of the "Belgian Waffle" -- a

combination of waffle, strawberries and whipped cream. Hey, look, there we are at the Belgian Waffle place.

Kane: there were so many good things to eat there, I am stuffed. Oh, well, what's next?

Doc: we have one more visit to make and then we are off to home for you, and on to the next problem that needs my attention. Let's get back to the "Door" and head out; it's a quick trip, 1972, and back to Bell Labs in Washington to see some of the things they are doing now to make the futuristic things you saw in the GE carousel of Progress. They reached the alley between abandoned buildings.

Doc used his cosmic flashlight and a blue door appeared on the side of one of the buildings. Kane opened it and they went in.

Kane took Elway out, gave him dinner, and took him out in the alley for his nightly constitutional.

Washington DC 1972

It's a Good Day for Meeting

The sound of the landing woke Kane up. He had had some very interesting dreams during his nap. He hoped to remember them. They might be helpful in the future.

Kane: Ok Doc, this does not look like the woods of Indiana. Where are we and why are we here?

Doc: Well, Kane, we are back in Washington DC, and its 1972. I know you are into C++ and I figured you would want to meet the guy who started it.

Kane: I use that now, that would be great.

Doc: Well his name is Bjarne Stroustrup. He works in the Bell Labs at Murray hill. That was the birth place of C and then UNIX

Doc: had brought the door to the alley side of an industrial building in Murry Hill.

Kane and Doc headed oue, leaving Elway to chew on some old slippers that had found earlier in the trip.

Dox used the cosmic flashlight to make the door invisible and they headed off to the office of Dr. Stroustrup. Kane was looking forward to this meeting. He had always wondered about the origins of C++.

As they walked thru the Lobby of the research building, Kane's attention was drawn to a model. It was the first transistor. It was a point-contact germanium device. Bell labs had invented it in 1947. Kane decided he had to check that out at the Library when he got back to Indiana 2015.

When they reached Dr, Stroustrup, he was working some calculations on the board in this office. He looked up when they entered, waved, but kept on writing symbols on the board in a most frenzied

manner. He finally finished, at least for the moment, and turned to greet them. A big smile came over his face.

Bjarne: Hey Doc, what brings you around here?

Doc: Bjarne, I'd like you to meet my friend Kane. I 'm giving him a trip so could see how the internet was developed. He's using C so I thought you might chat with him a bit.

Bjarne: Hi Kane, glad to meet you. I'm at a good point to take a break. Have a chair. I won't ask any questions, I know that Doc knows people from ALL over.

Kane: thanks, Can you tell me what drove C and what are the ground rules for its continued development? How do you know when it's time for changes?

Bjarne: There are a few rules that govern how C develops.

First it's only driven by real problems, and should be useful right away in real world problems. We do not make changes without a need.

Second, every feature should be implementable with a reasonably obvious way to do it.

Third, It should provide facilities for combining organizing programs into well-defined parts and provide facilities for combining separately developed parts.

And Fourth, it should co—exist with other programming languages rather than having its own separate and incompatible programming environment.

There are other rules, but these general guidelines are what we use to upgrade features and functionality of C.

Kane: I see that, it makes perfect sense. That makes it easier to grow with it, instead of having to learn everything from scratch.

Bjarne: Well guys, I've got to get back to the effort, I happened to get a flash of an idea while we were chatting, and I want to work it in.

With that he turned back to the blackboard, totally absorbed in the new modification he wanted to add.

Doc and Kane quietly left and headed back to the alley wall that had parked the door at.

Elway was thrilled to see them; he was hungry and fully awake. He went to the shelf and found a new supply of dog food and chicky feet treats. He fed Elway and the took him out for his normal constitutional. He did get a few treats while he was out. He and Kane had bonded on the trip and Kane was working some new tricks with Elway. It would be a real surprise to every one back home.

It's a Good Day for a Trip in Time and Space

Kane went to the window; He never tired of the eternally changing view. Oh, this must be just like it looks to the astronauts. It would be neat meet some of the NASA space pioneers; what stories they could tell. Now the view had changed;

According to Doc, it was the Angel Nebula... It was beautiful. Then the view changed again; the stars were so beautiful.

He wished Doc was nearby so he could ask the name of this star cluster.

Doc was in the Apartment, or maybe taking a swim in the indoor pool this Space-Time travel vehicle was loaded with options. It had a number of apartments, Kane and Elway had their own place and a robotic cleaner picked things up almost faster than they could put it down. The clothes were instantly transported to the cleaning device and in 5 minutes it was cleaned, pressed and hung up or put on a shelf in his apartment. It had a DNA detector, so it knew who it belonged to, and knew where it should be stored. He was impressed, but he really was not used to having his socks ironed.

Washington DC 1992

It's a Good Day for a Meeting

Doc: Kane, this is a special day. We are on our way to the Senate Office Building. We have a meeting with Senator Al Gore. You know they say he invented the internet.

Kane: Sure, I've heard that: usually being joked about by late night comedians. But are you sure about this? He's likely to throw us out.

Doc: You think so, ok, so if that's the worst that can happen, then why not ask? You might be surprised by what he tells you.

Kane: Ok, you have not steered me wrong so far. Elway is sleeping so it's a good time to go.

It takes a few minutes to get there; they had left the door in a side alley a block away from the Senate Office Building. (SOBs for short).

They were greeted by one of Senator Gore's staff.

Hi Doc, welcome to Washington. The Senator is expecting you, go on in.

Doc: Hi Senator, It's good to see you again. It's been a while.

He got up and walked around his desk and shook hands with Doc:

Al: So who is this young man with you?

Doc: This is Kane, a friend of mine. He is studying the evolution of the internet, and I suggested he meet the man who invented it.

Al: Oh you did, did you? (chuckling)

Kane: Actually he want me to ask you about that?

Al: well, it was one of those times when I was not quite as exact as I probably should have been... I was talking political dialogue to a news guy who didn't understand the language. Here is the background and what I really said.

In the 1980s, I promoted legislation that funded an expansion of the ARPANET, allowing greater public access, and helping to develop the Internet.

I had been involved with computers since the 1970s, first as a Congressman and later as Senator and Vice President, where I was a genuine nerd, with a geek reputation running back to my days as a futurist *Atari Democrat* in the House. Before computers were understood, I actually tried to explain artificial intelligence and fiber-optic networks to my colleagues, but most of them fell asleep in the middle of the best parts. Public usage of the Internet was limited but the problem of giving ordinary Americans network access had excited me since the late 1970s.

In 1986, I introduced Senate Bill 2594 *Supercomputer Network Study Act of 1986* And we began to put together the *High Performance Computing and Communication Act of 1991*

Doc: Kane, this was commonly referred to as "The Gore Bill".

In fact, a UCLA professor of computer science, Leonard Kleinrock, one of the central creators of the ARPANET (the ARPANET, first deployed by Kleinrock and others in 1969, is the predecessor of the Internet) would later credit both Gore and the *Gore Bill* as a critical moment in Internet history:

Al: I then promoted legislation that resulted in President George H.W Bush signing the *High Performance Computing and Communication Act of 1991*. This Act allocated $600 million for high performance computing and for the creation of the *National Research and Education Network* . The NREN brought together industry, academia and government in a joint effort to accelerate the development and deployment of gigabit/sec networking.

Doc: (In an aside to Kane) The bill was passed on Dec. 9, 1991 and led to the National Information Infrastructure (NII) Perhaps one of the most important results of the Gore Bill was the development of Mosaic in 1993. This World Wide Web browser is credited by most scholars as beginning the Internet boom of the 1990s**.**

Kane: In my own terms, you were the nerd in the Senate who had a vision of giving access to everyone and put together an Appropriation to fund the research and the development of the structure to allow the Internet to become available all of us.

Al: Yep, you got it.

Kane: Thanks for the insight. It's a far different picture that you see on the late night talk shows. I guess it pays to do your own verification of what the news medias tell you.

Doc: It sure is Kane, it is important to listen to balance views on all topics, and then do your own research to see how events will impact you.

A Good Day for a Trip in Time and Space

They continued the conversation, with Kane relating some of his efforts and Al seemed genially interested. After a goodbye handshake, they left the office and headed back to the alley. They needed to get back; it had been an interesting adventure. Kane wondered if Doc would make the time slice he had promised, or would he have to have a good reason for being missing. Oh well, time would tell…

Doc turned, used his cosmic flashlight, and the door appeared.
Doc, and Kane opened the door, stepped inside and with a Vrrrfffff, Vrrrfffff, Vrrrfffff… Time seems to stand still. The door is gone.

Cooper: Well the shadow is almost there, Rupert.
Rupert: Yea, I know, well, we better get ready, they will be back soon. He's never been late coming back here.

Suddenly they hear: Vrrrfffff, Vrrrfffff, Vrrrfffff… Time seems to stand still. They look at each other.

Cooper: Yep, yep, yep; Here they are, it's that timey whimey whatis guy coming back again.

A large door appears in the clearing in the midst of a bright light. Kane, and Elway step out in to the clearing,
Kane: Wow, what a trip. And I can't tell anyone, either, they will think I am crazy… no one can go back in history. Was it all a dream… Hmm, I'll have to go to the library and check this all out. But why him I talking to you dogs, you don't understand what I am saying anyway.

Rupert and Cooper looked at each other and smiled that smile that dogs have when they know they are smarter than you are.

They head back down to the cottage, and they are just in time for dinner; it was a cookout on the deck.

Grampa Ed: Well Kane, how was your hike up the trail. Anything unusual happen?
Kane: Nope, everything was just as always, peaceful and quiet.

Well, now, people say that dogs don't understand human speech, but…
Elway gave Kane the strangest look, and you could hear Rupert and Cooper making little chuckling noises, but then again, perhaps they could and just didn't want us to know…

www.ingramcontent.com/pod-product-compliance
Lightning Source LLC
Chambersburg PA
CBHW041148050326
40689CB00001B/528